In Time I Am

Isabelle Athmann

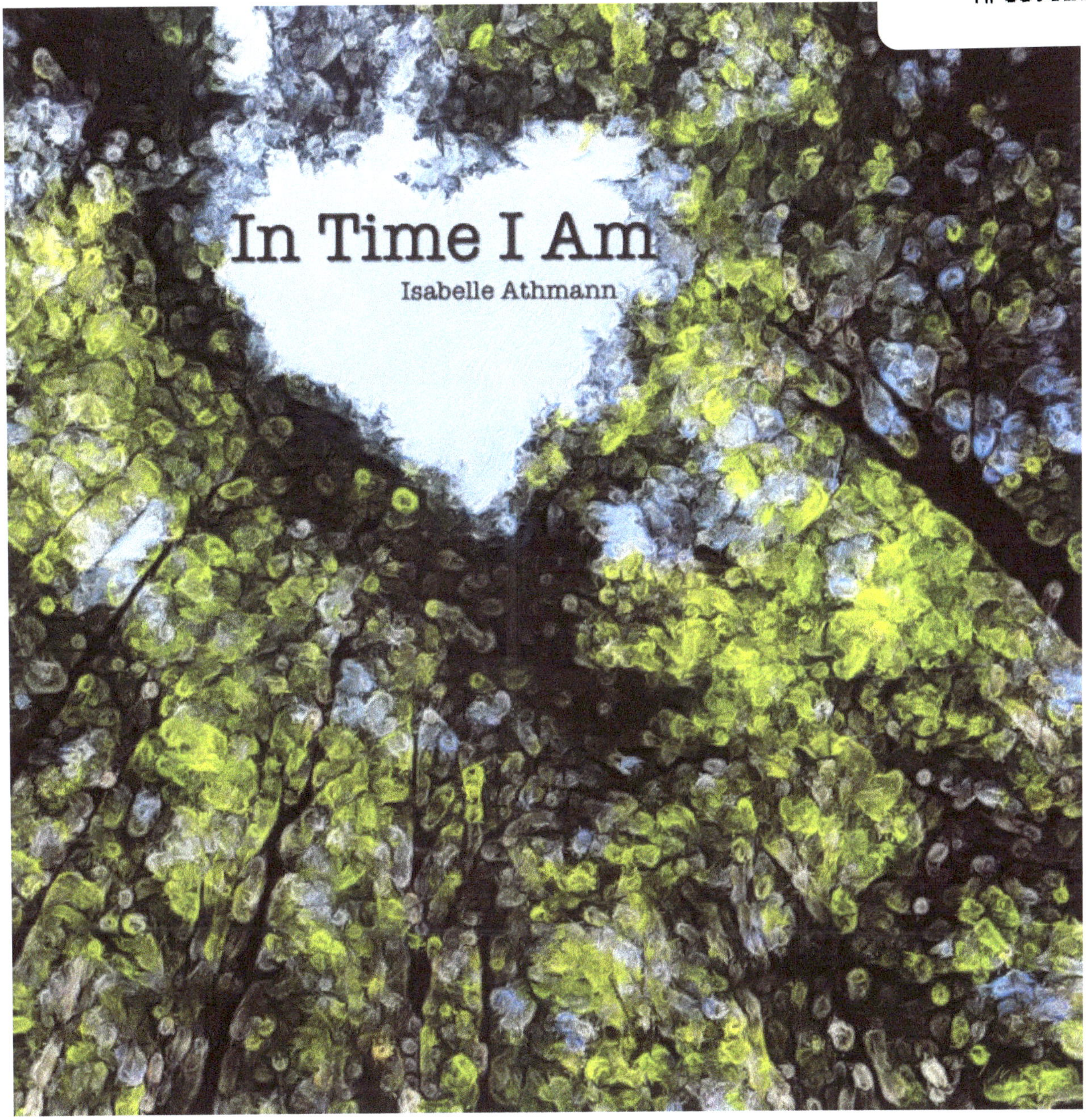

ISBN 978-1-716-01864-0

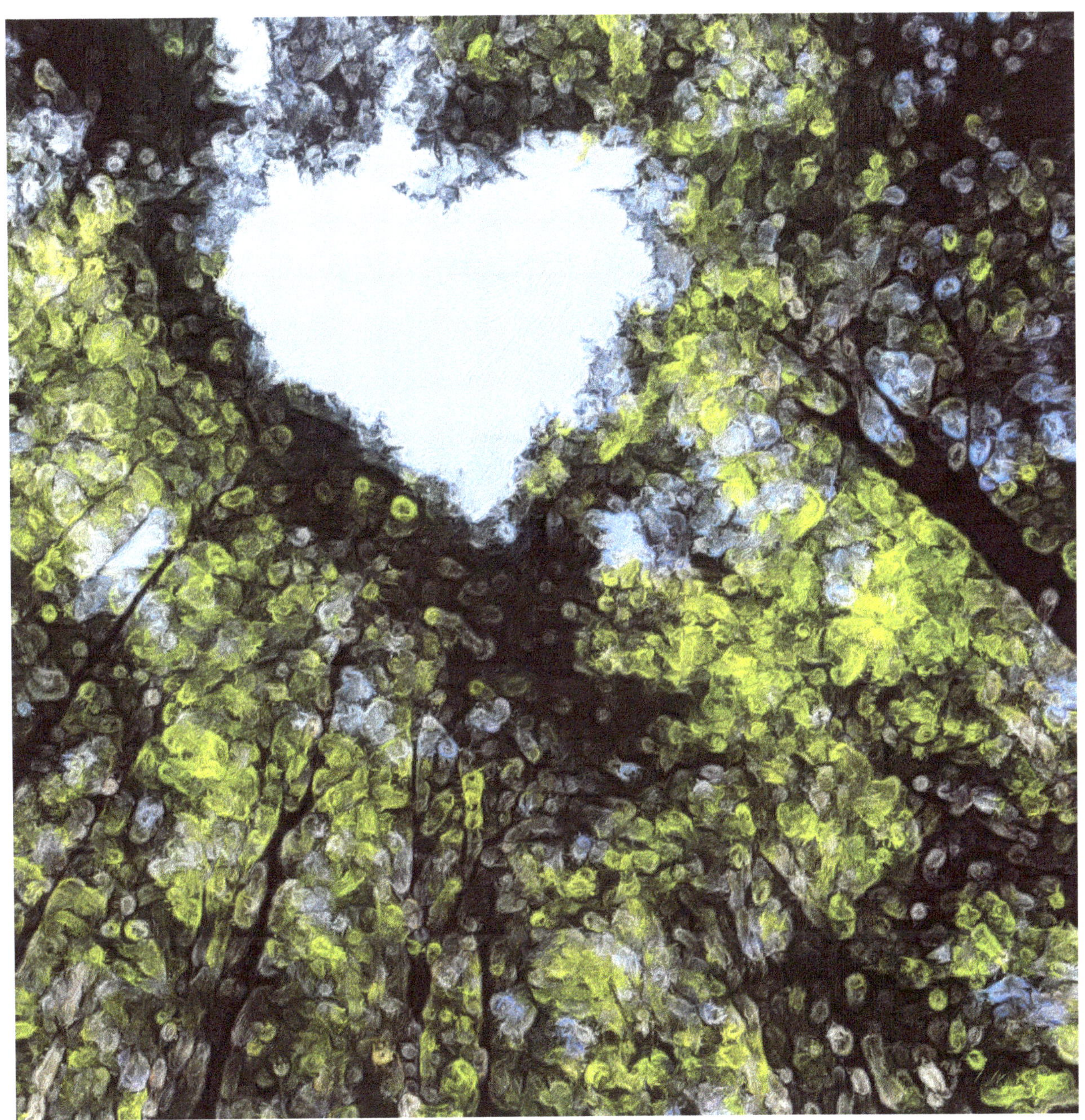

dedication

to the kind hopefuls
those knights and saints who live by
God's wish and command

Introduction

This is a brave book. Within is a reflection of years of acquired knowledge. Obtained by bringing memories forward and reflecting actual mastery of the gently earned awareness. Knowledge is attained by being the very presence of kindness. I write as a poet, conservationist, and Reiki master. Combined, this ascended genius put in words is meant for the brave-hearted. Hope is to further foster the witnessed gentleness of time. My verse may trigger your own memories. Tender forward all appearances and expressions of enlightenment. I can attest attainment of the illumination of comprehension is possible. For reverence of all of life has always been the intended rhythm and rhyme of the ages. I encourage the reader to nourish your own inner nature of actual benevolence and authentic goodwill.

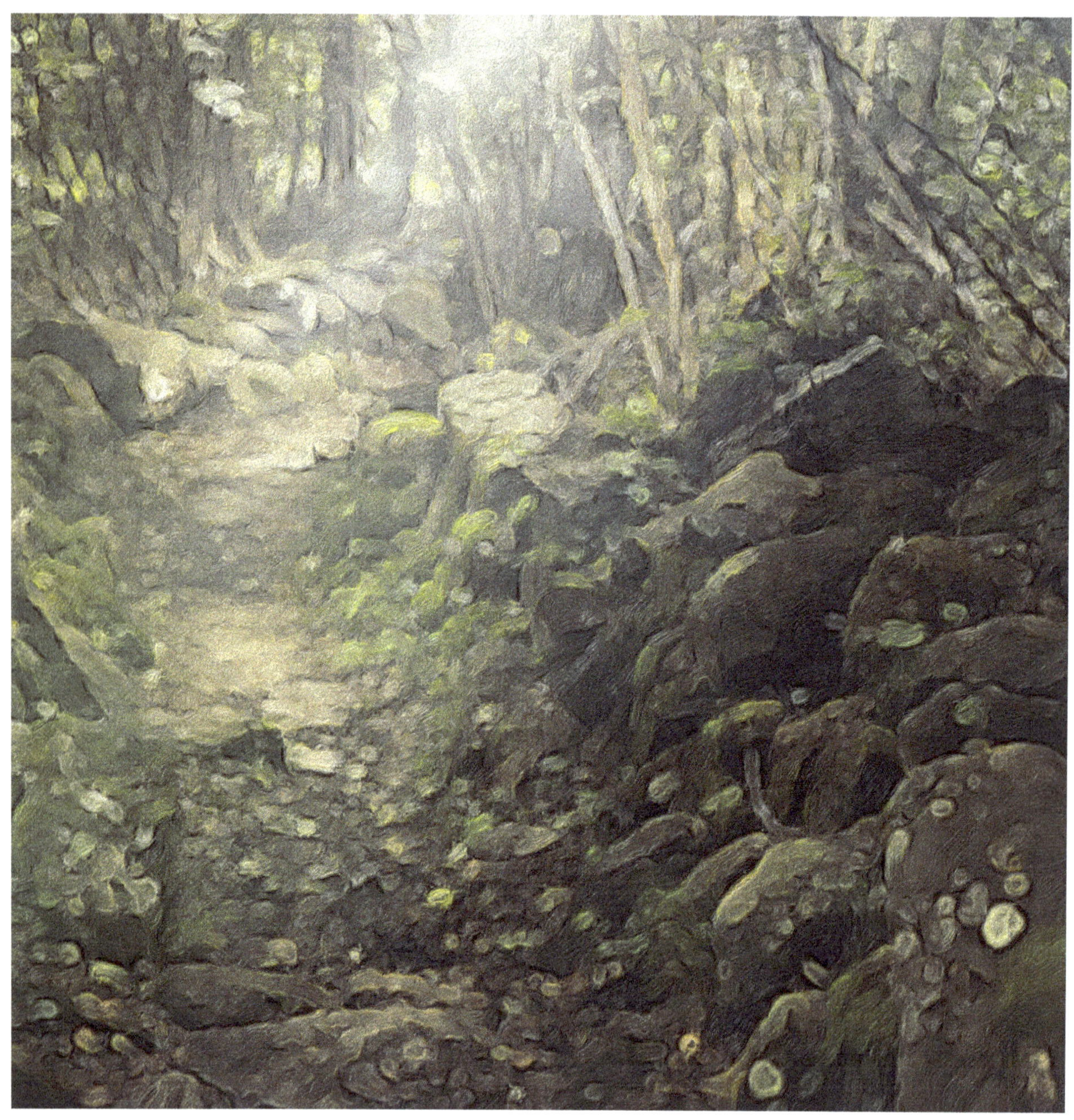

I am in light of the yonder of wonder
that which causes the traveler in me.
I even like the broken-in path, for the trait
of preservation is a travelers gain.

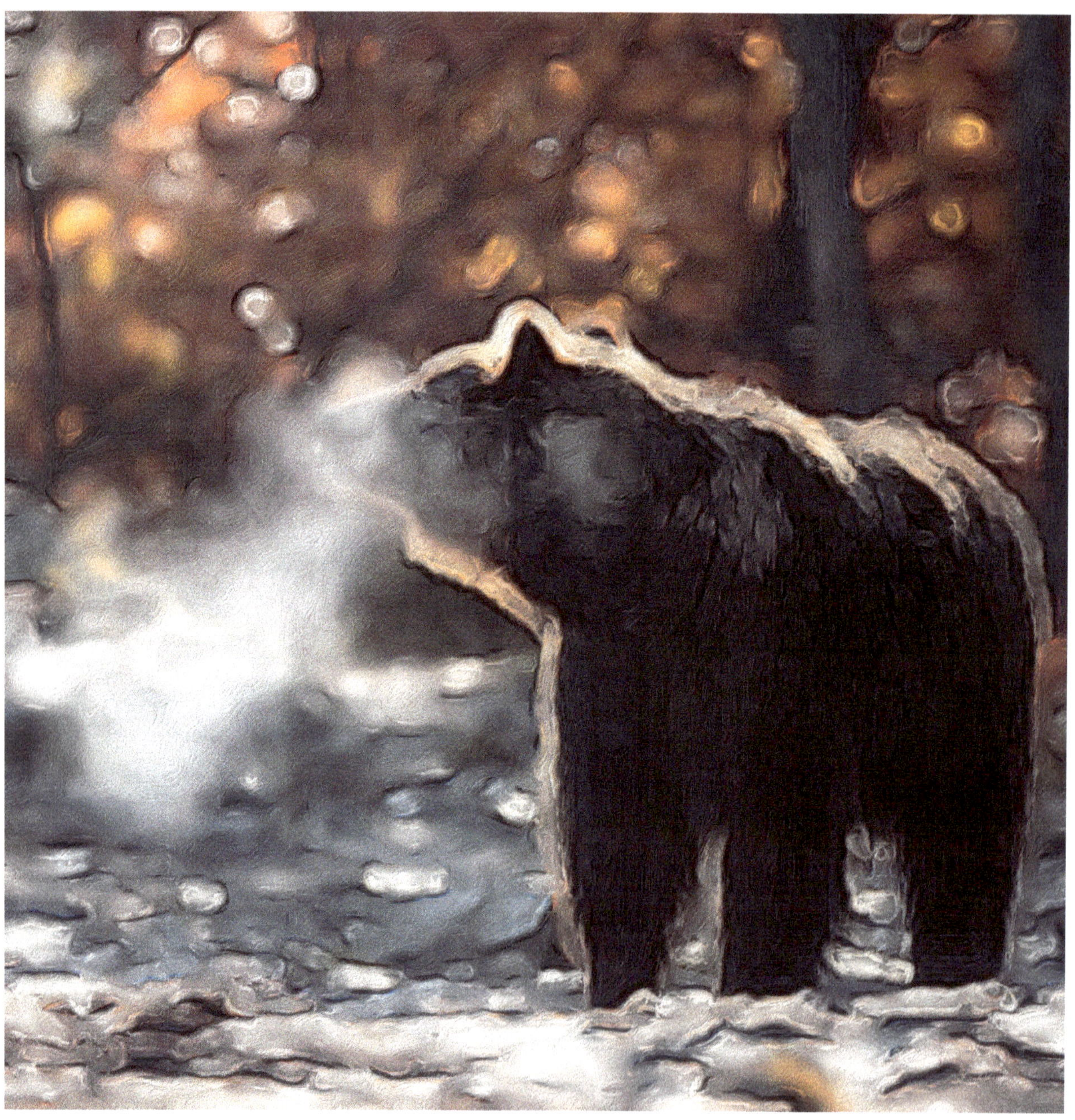

There is no experience in which
the reward is greater than
within the preservation of a breath.
We are all companions on this journey
to like our existence and experiences.

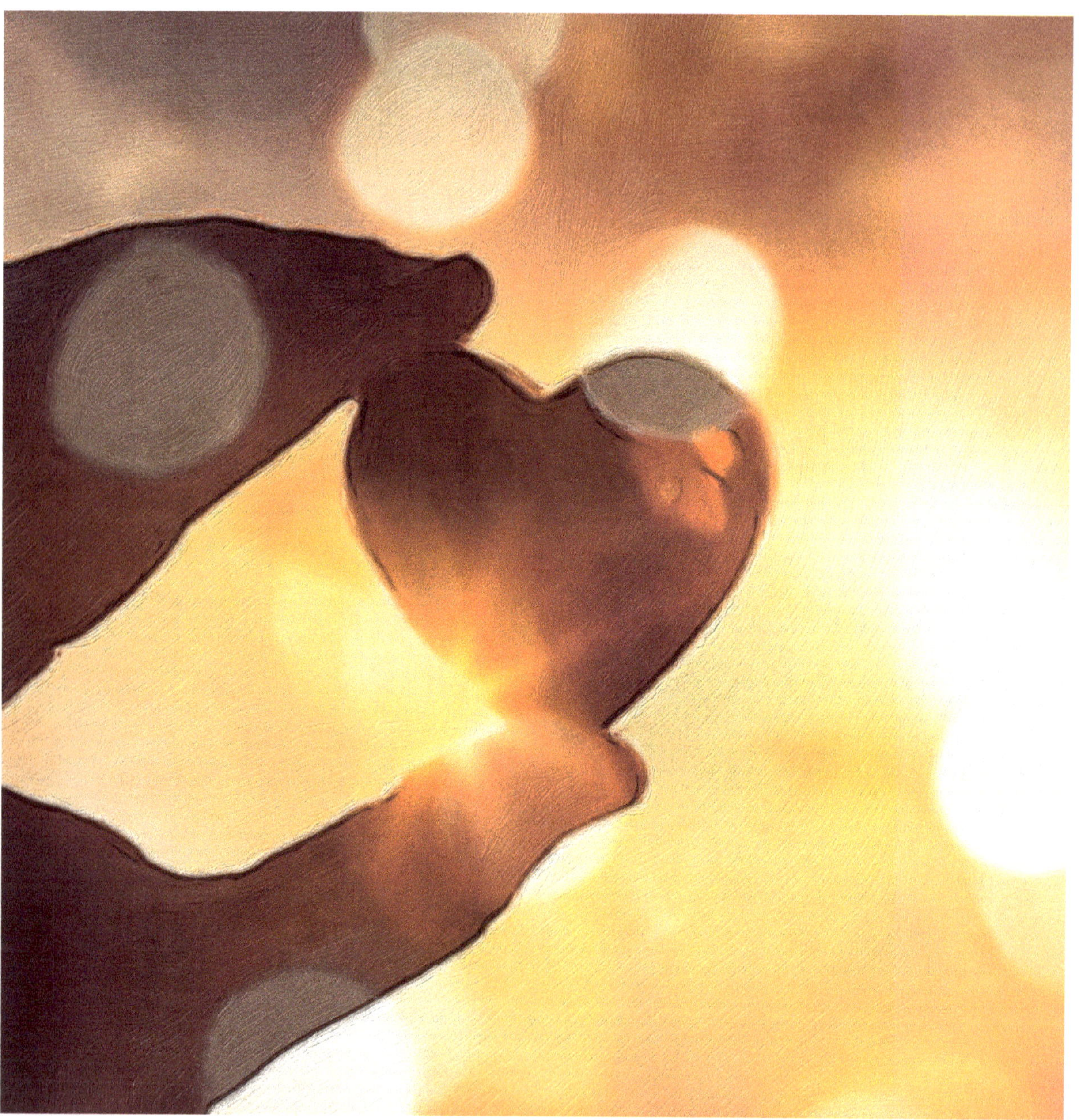

I am held in the innocence of God's accounting,
for any perceived debts have been remunerated
through my cumulative acts of kindness.

In time I am breath in glory,
for the guiding light does inspire through the
preciousness of breath, the Heaven of our
beingness, all forms of bravery and kindness.

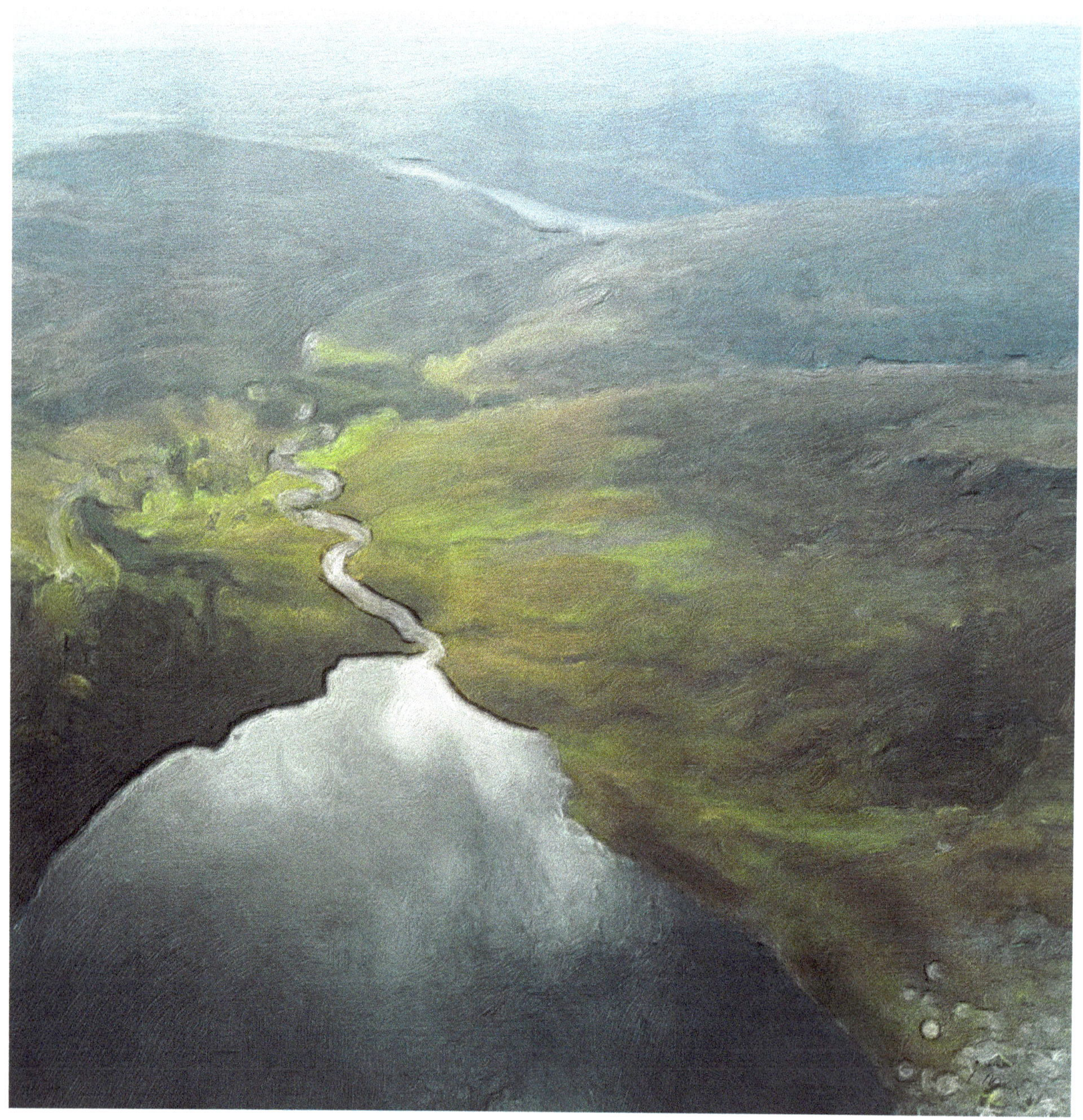

There is no place like home
and forever the land takes that claim
although the sea was the beginning here.

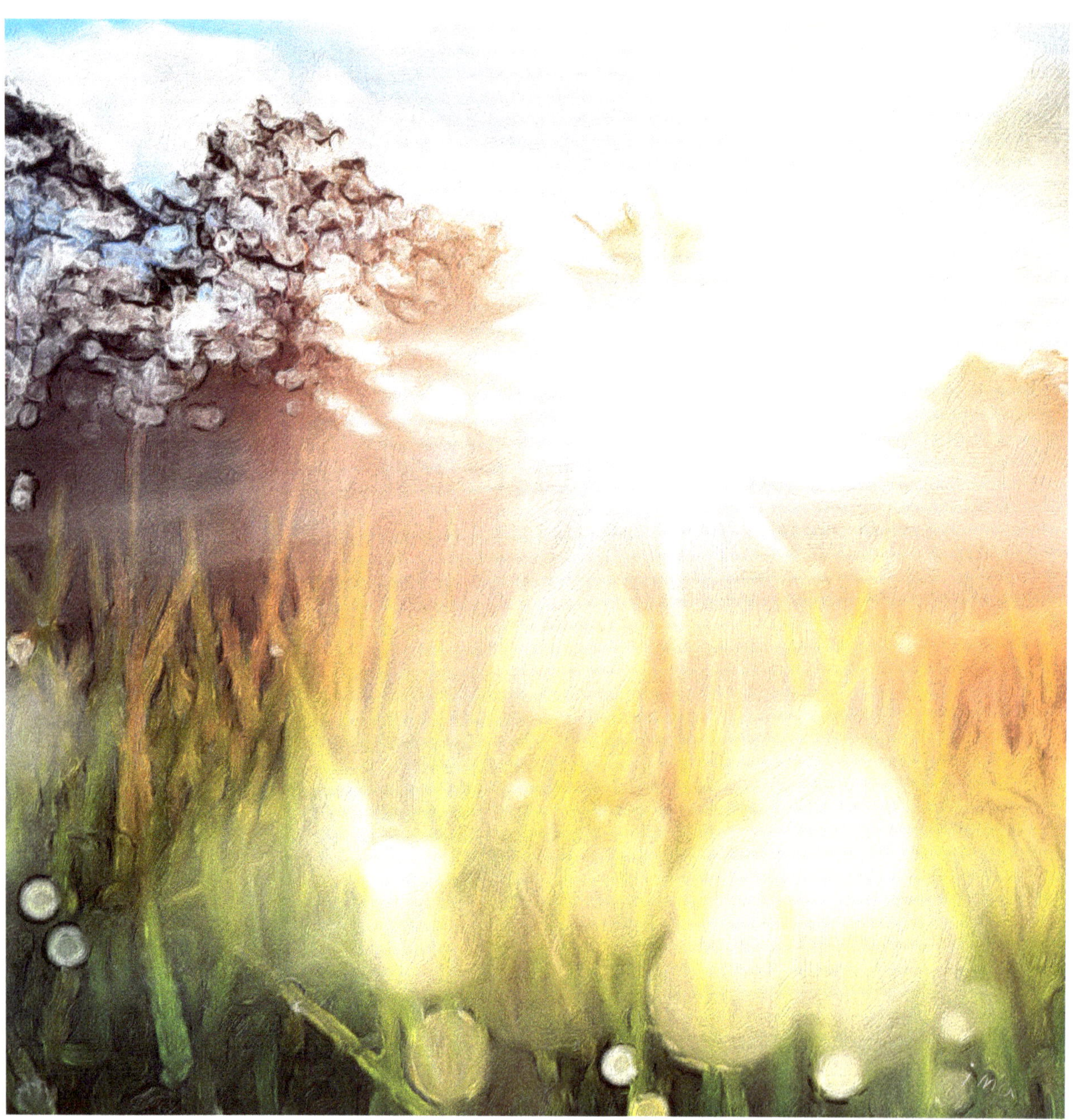

In time I am a blessing, blessing,
for I am in the hope that peace
is what guides us forever, forever.

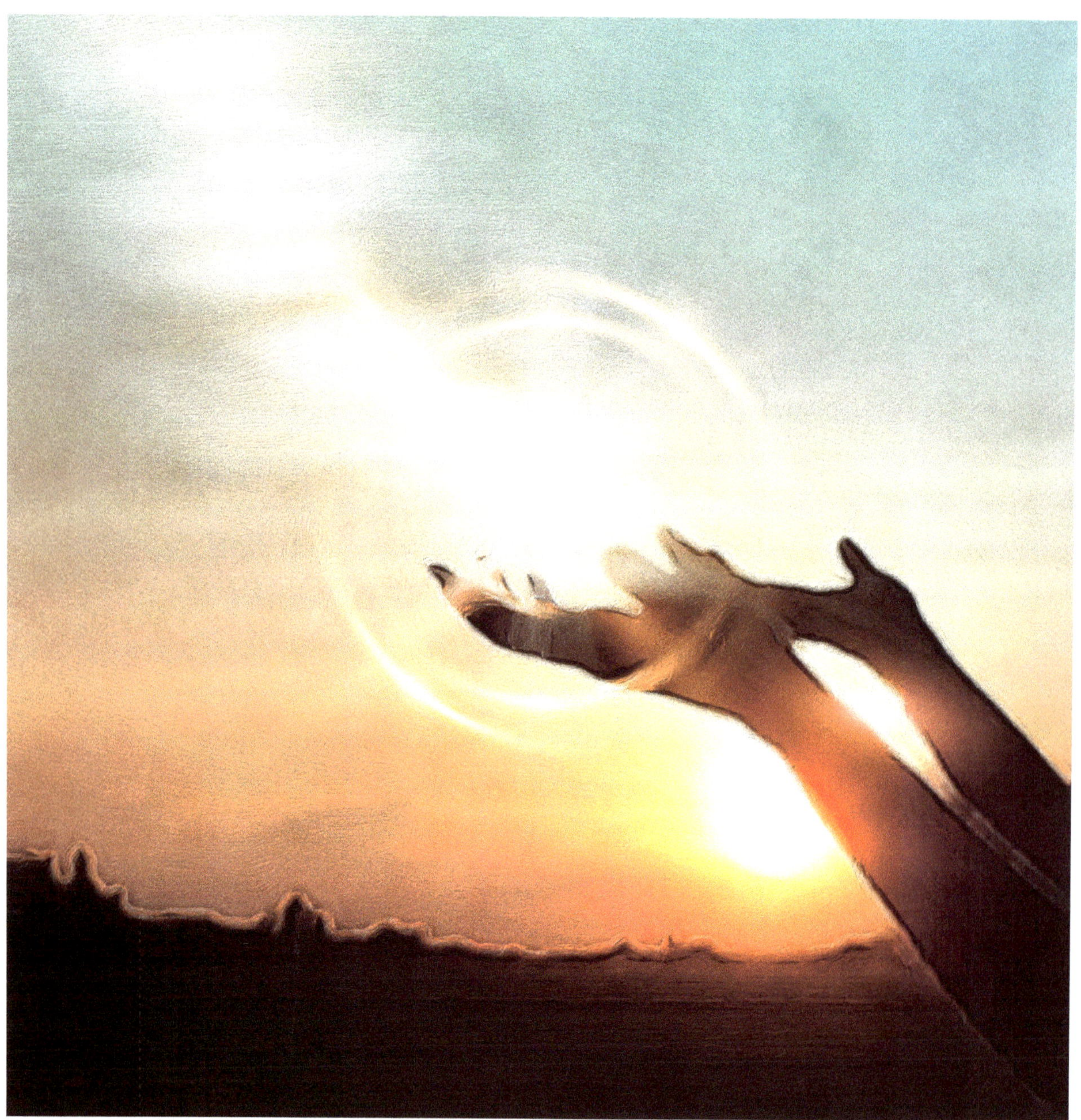

There should always
be a rhythm to call peace home,
that forever hopeful pulse
that send us to prayer. Today,
tomorrow, and yesterday
for even I have discerned it.

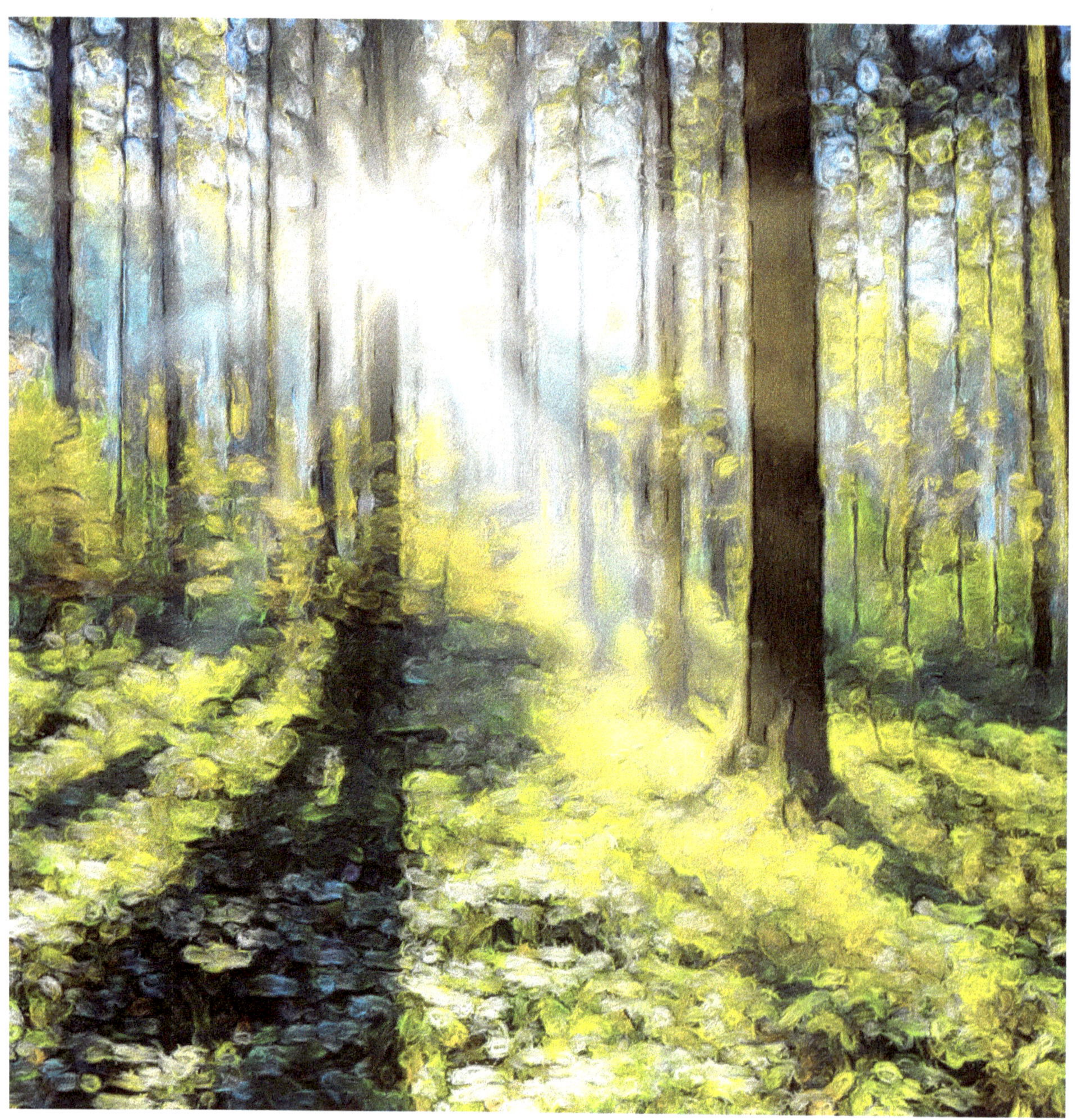

Being in glory is in being the very reflection of the kindness of God's numerous graces. For example, God's breath of his enchanting natural world, his elegant wilderness, and ever his hopeful wildness.

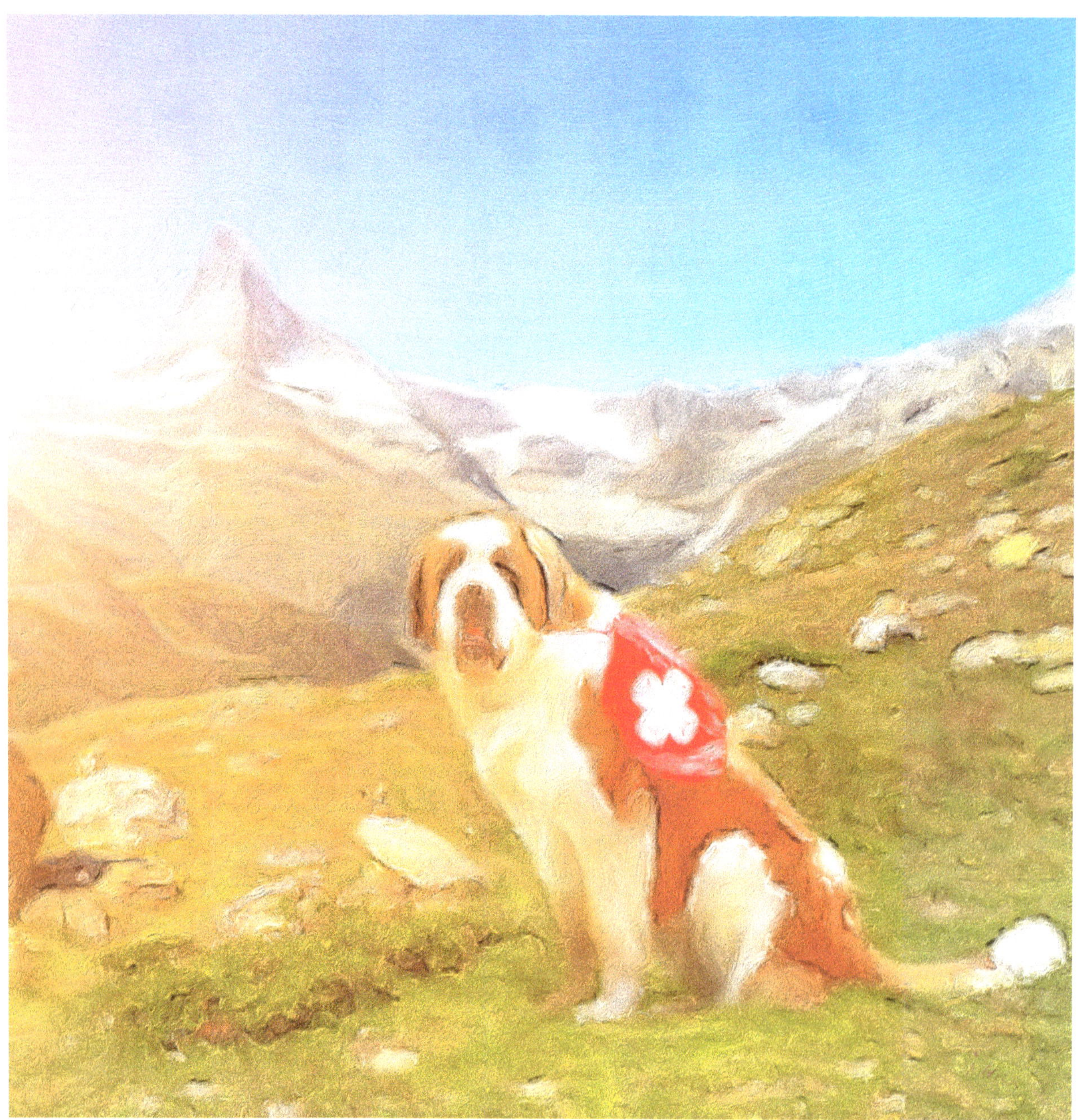

Heaven is the care and concern bestowed to others it is saving the life and hope of another. Then Jesus said, "heaven is breathing." For I was there.

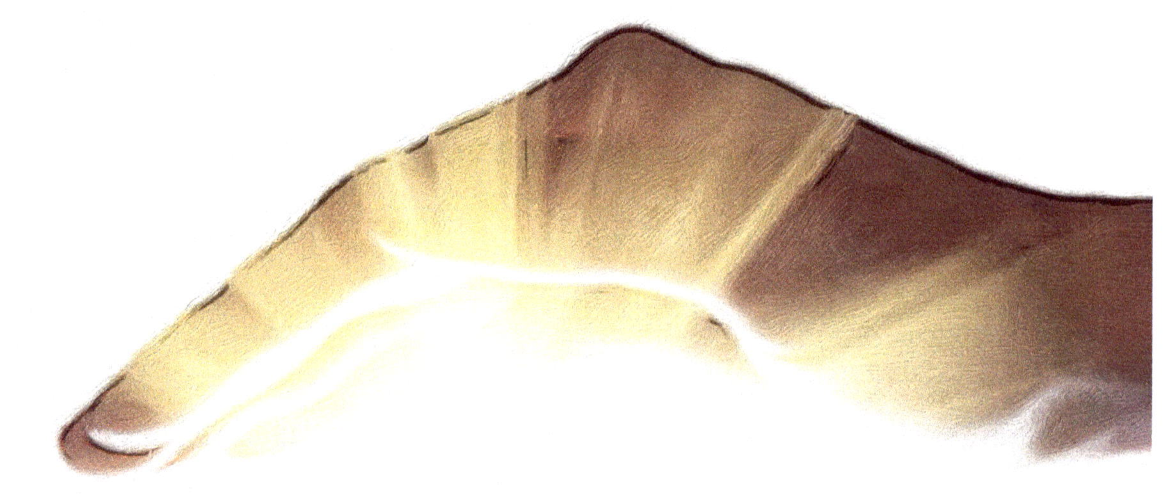

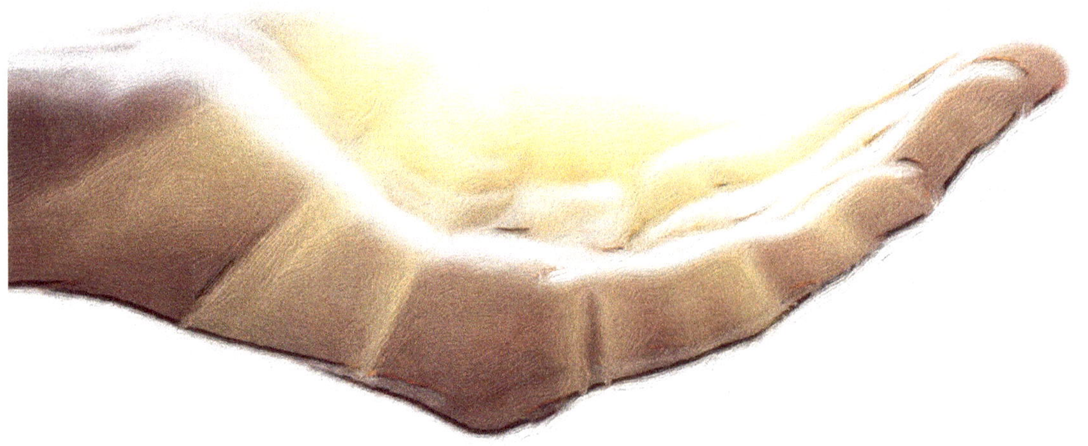

I am hopeful that the kindness
I was granted, that wise pulse, is always
inherited. For I have seen it in myself,
as well in the very nature of others.
And intend to always express
its avenue, channel its awareness,
and marvel at its wisdom.

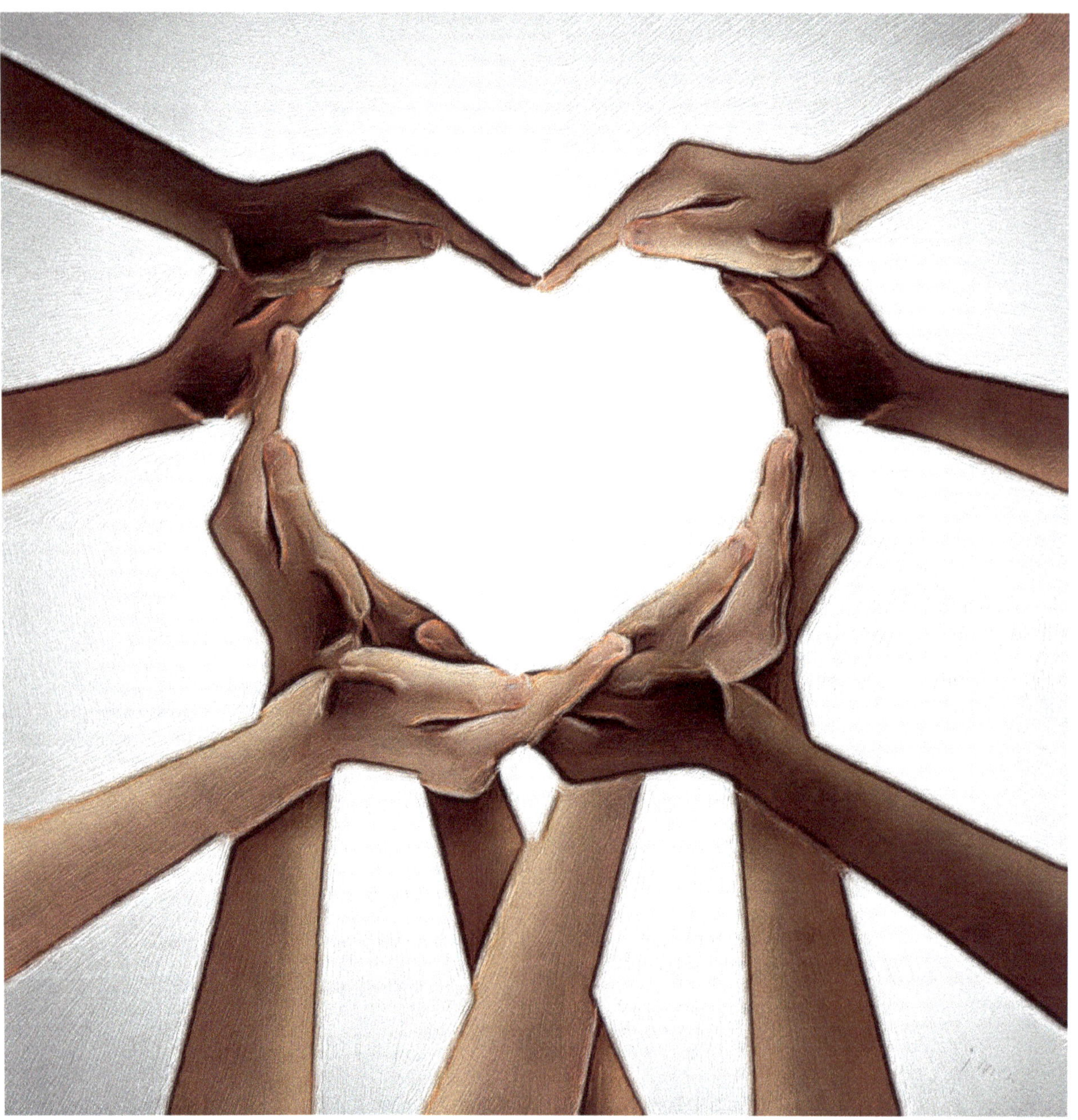

For glory's conclusive definition is
in the wisdom of kindness, compassion,
and the courage to show this empathy.

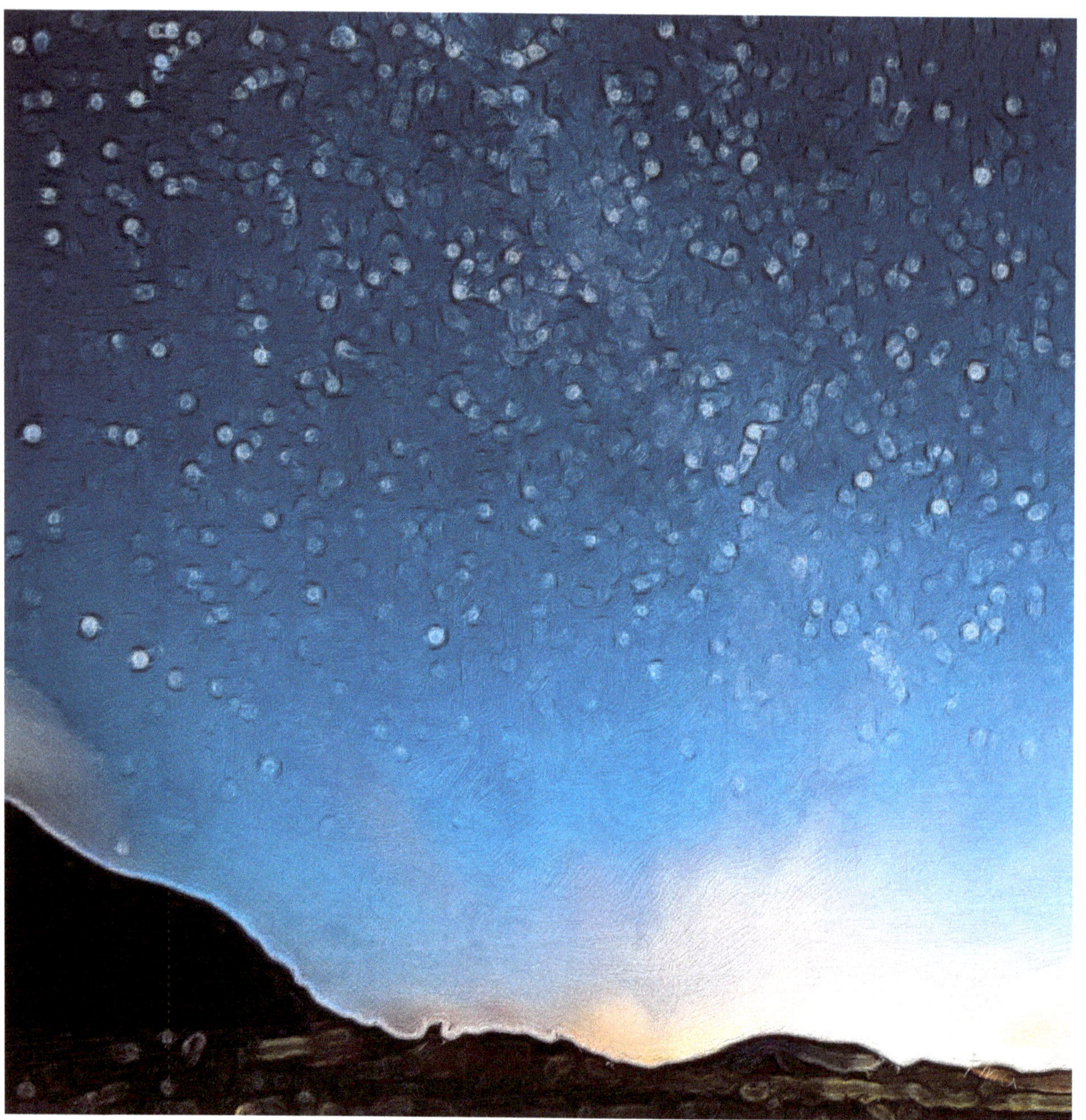

Be forever kind. Knowing those acts of compassion are graciously witnessed and recorded by those who guide us. Chronicled by the Cosmos of dreams and visions sent and seen. Our wise council is the Camelot of Hope.

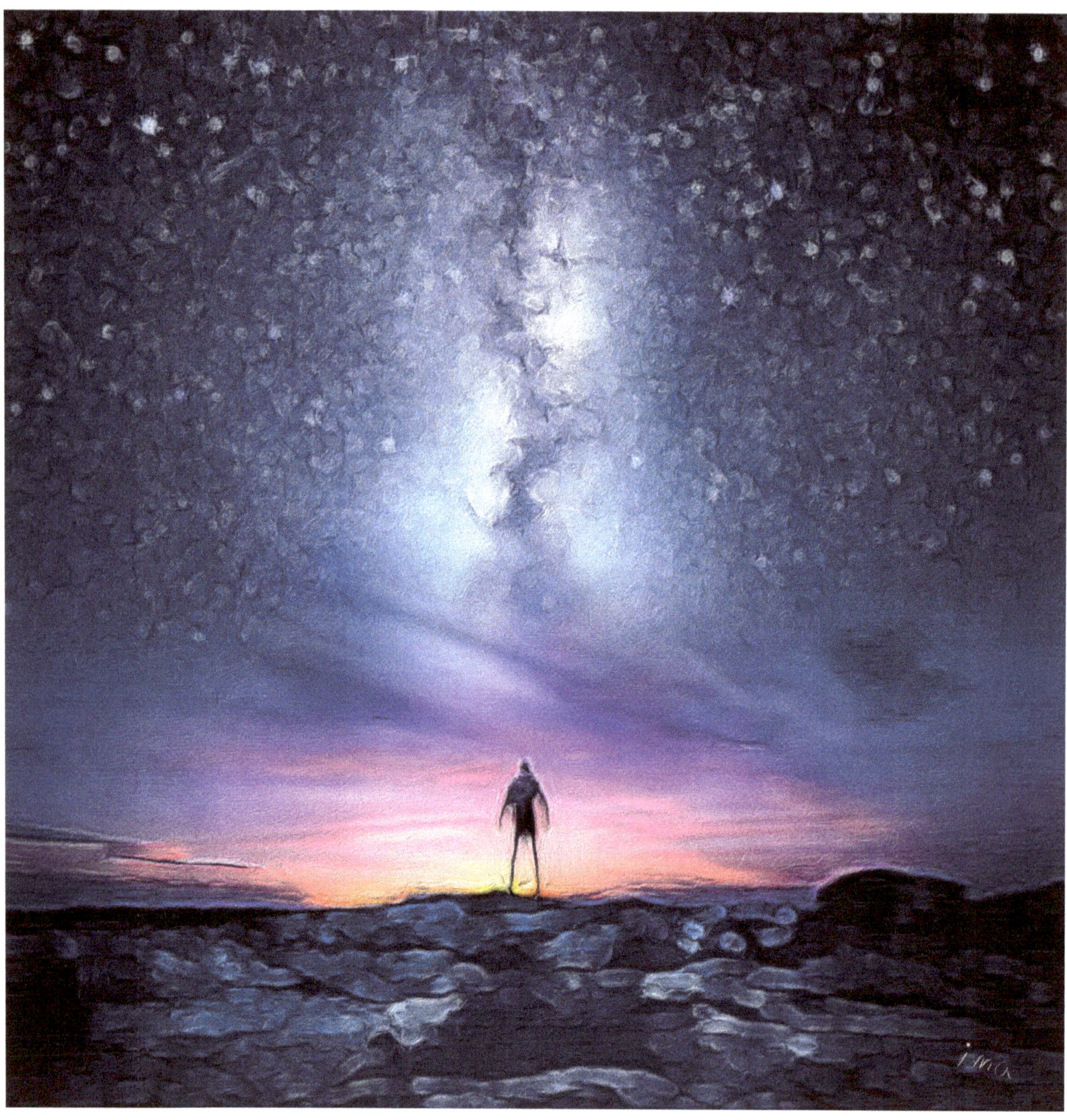

I am at glory's beckoning to be the kindness I
know God is, and his beacon Zeus,
that twin of discernment and courage.
Enchanted, I am with both.

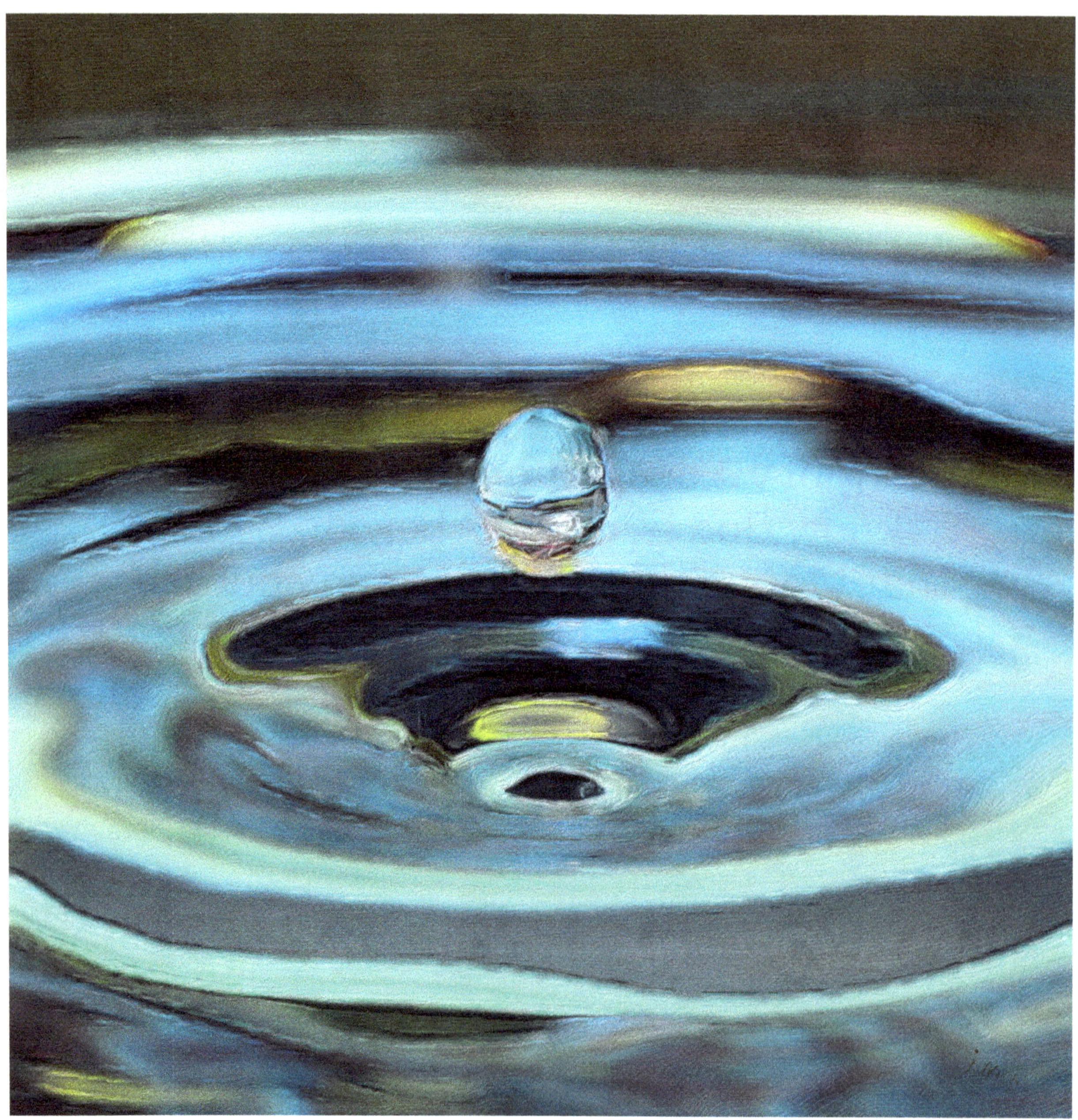

Forever God has been the very pulse of kindness. So, in turn, our own tuning fork is to forever reflect back his stately wave within all our actions. So this ripple has been. Since time's beginning and to be carried to all forevers.

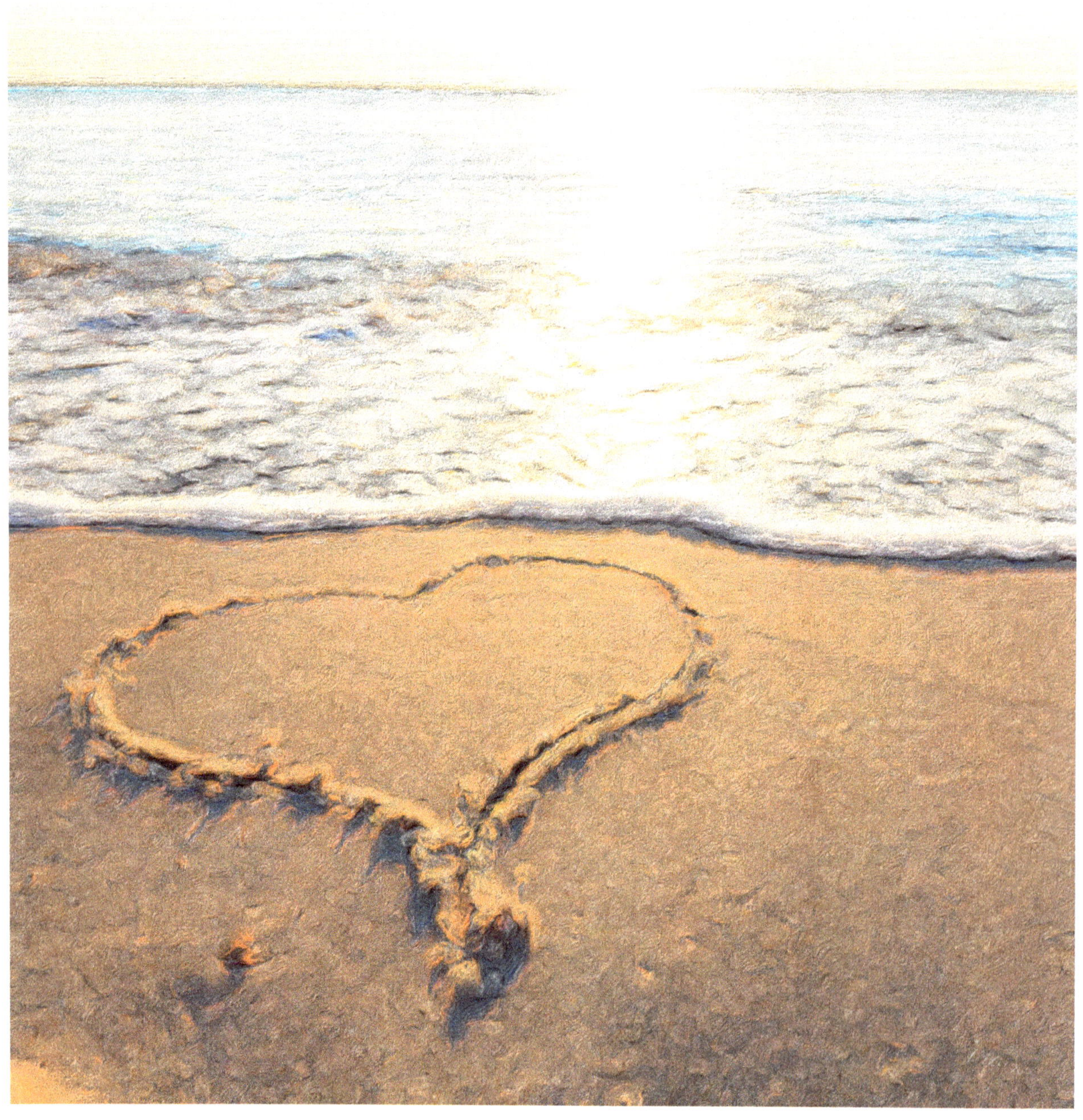

Foresight is attainable. Merely empathically care and concern oneself with tending to the needs of Padre's creatures of the day and night. Then, evenly apply this Reiki wisdom.

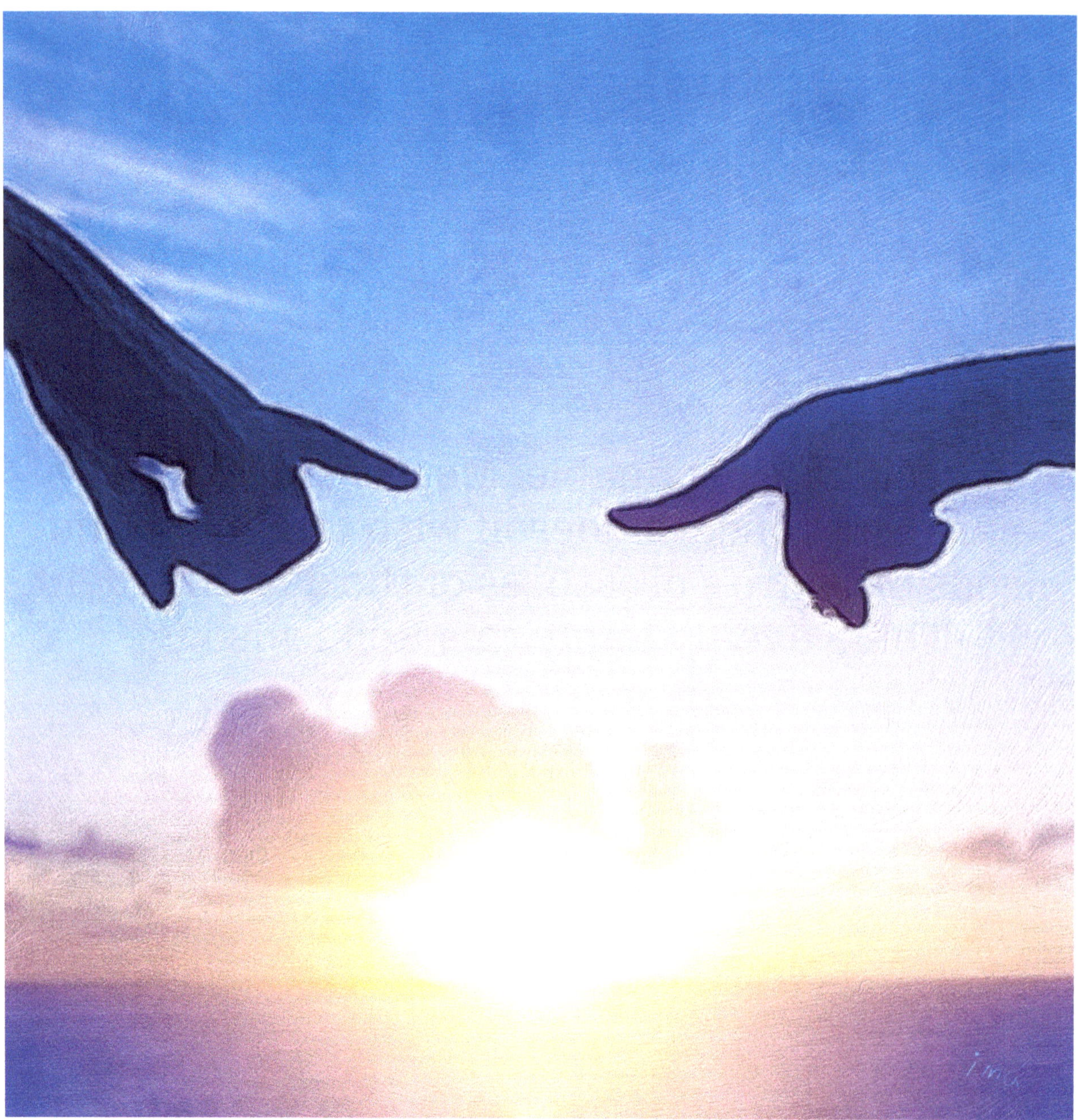

In time I am not you. Nor the projections you
place on us. Those feign concern. We are of Reiki
wisdom, deep in the knowledge that your false
tales directed towards us are not about us and
never will be. So may we be free of these
incorrect fathomless estimations as they merely
protest their own self-hatred at us.
We are not them, and our discernment
is no longer in the background.

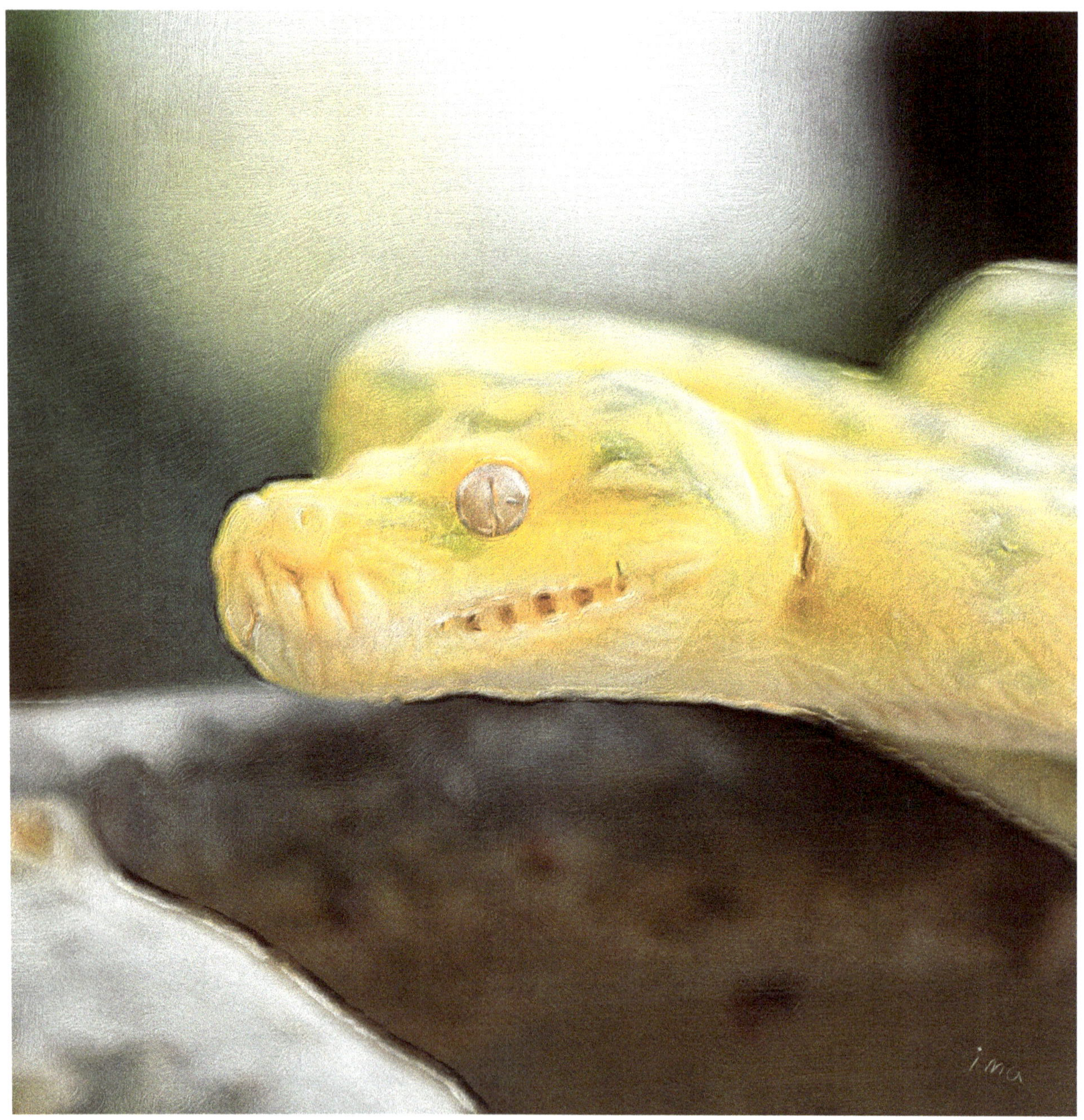

There was a snake within the Garden of Eden,
so wise as to remark for us to "consume
nourishment from various plant sources." The
Tree of Knowledge was the pomegranate, which
is self-evident that the snake was right.
Vegetation is our birthright to sustain us.
The heartbeat was meant to be
left alone to their own stellar devices.

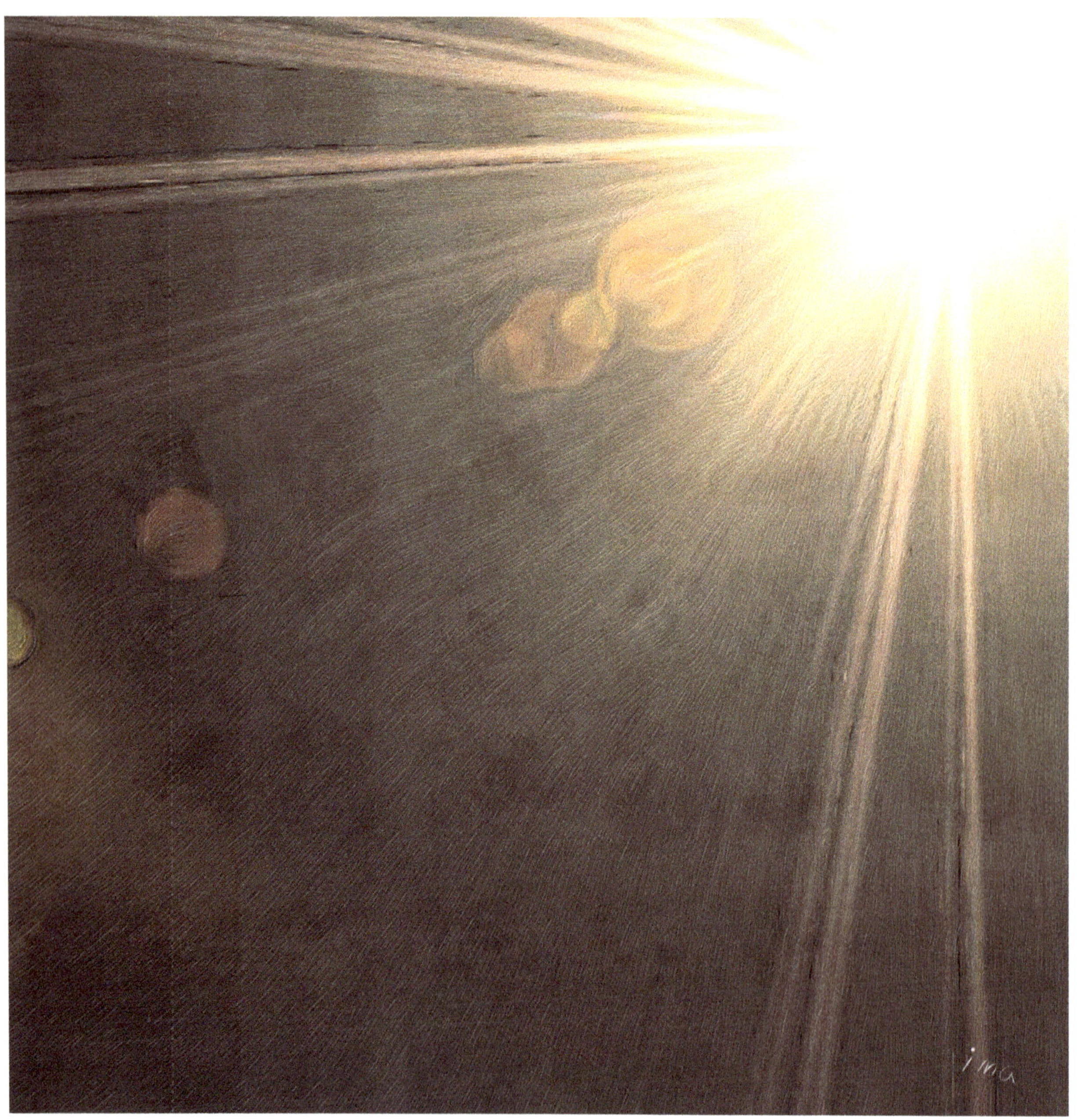

Life's web weaves optimism and cries
for gentle kindness. So, naturally,
our expectations are to like both.

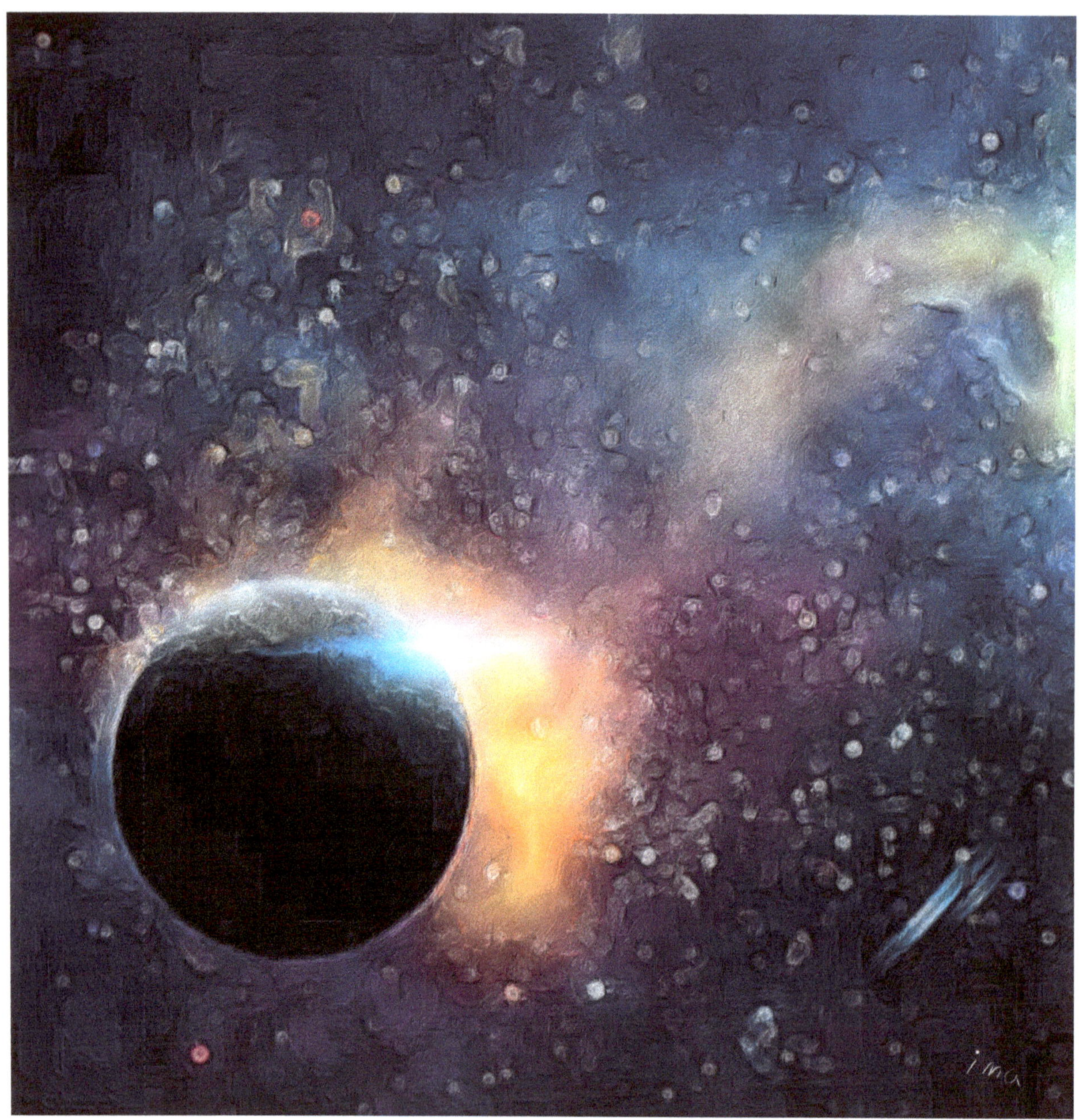

Enlightenment is a badge of knowledge that we are all connected to "I am the Light." Designed to be kind, even the darkness. We quake in fear that it appears at times not so.

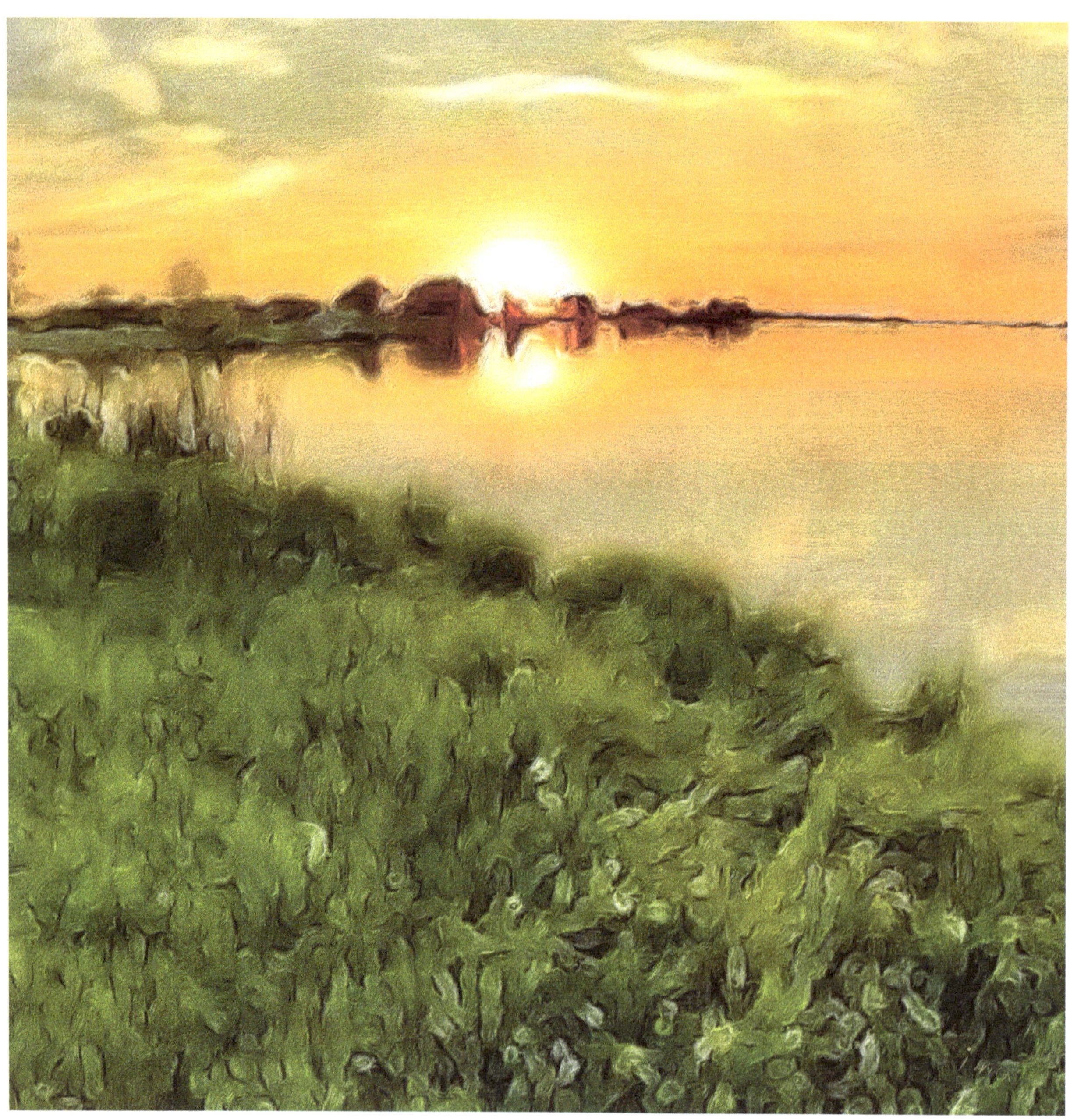

At the water's edge of time,
I witnessed numerous acts of kindness and
traveled that wisdom landward all lifetimes. So
to have you. Kindness's goodwill, those
accumulating acts of courage were
always intended to be forever, forever.

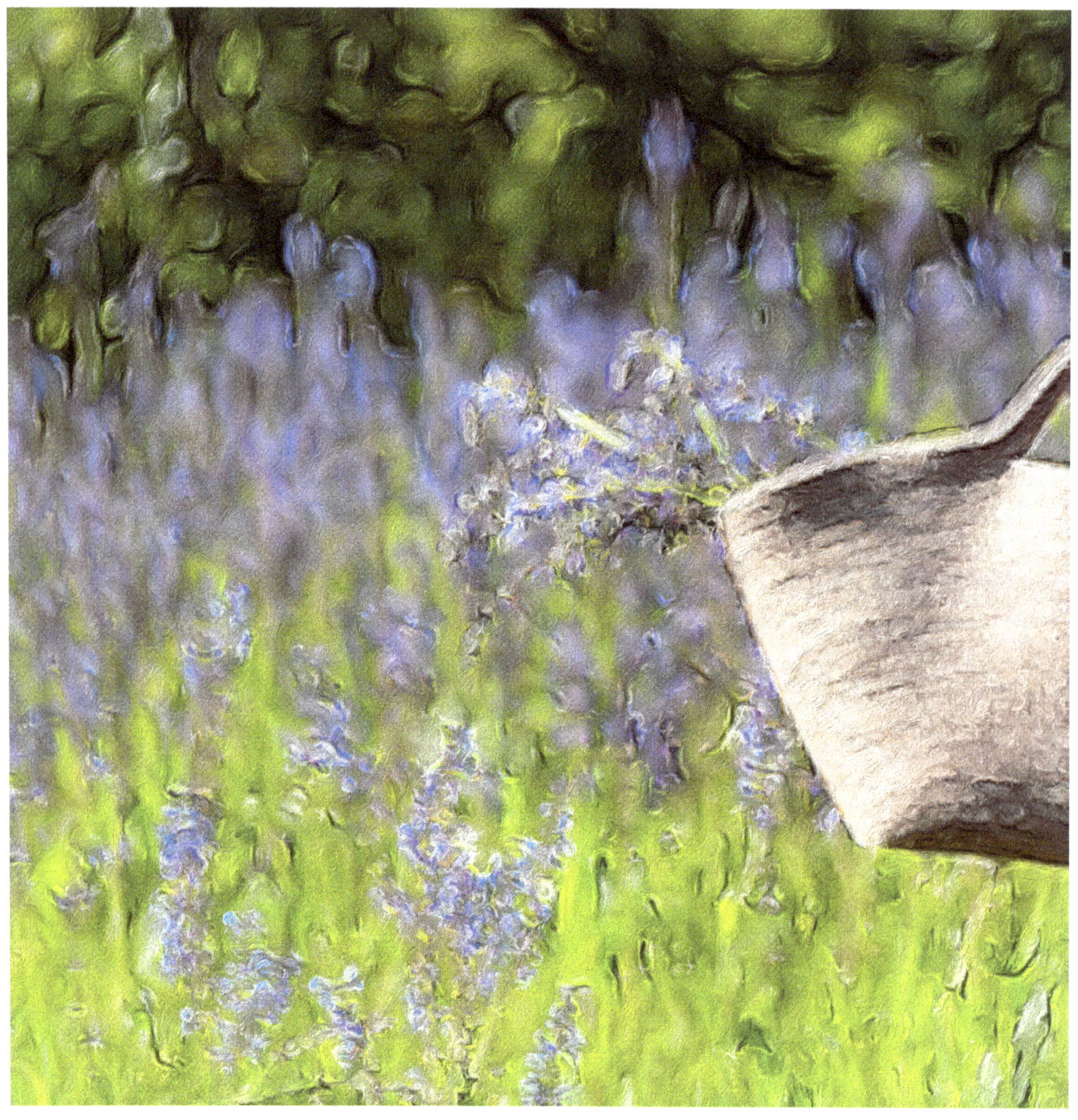

To Note

Narnia had been foretold by the Jesus of our stars. Then again, as Buddha. Their journey was to deliver a feather to the stag. The Latin I am familiar with has no verse that hurts. Hunter, hunter, used to connote weaving a basket for the assigned fruit. A fruitful basket for the chaff of corn, wheat, grass, grain, flowering herbs, and tree harvests. Then abundance is acknowledged. Those painted arrows appeared much later. Safari in Latin was to see ourselves in the beauty of God's creatures; it meant discern mirror. Latin definition of holiness was restoration. Many are surprised to wake up to the current crisis. The brave speak out and act altruistically, for their shepherd is their well-intended and noble consciousness. Reiki in Latin meant guiding light hand of hope, be a conduit of peace.

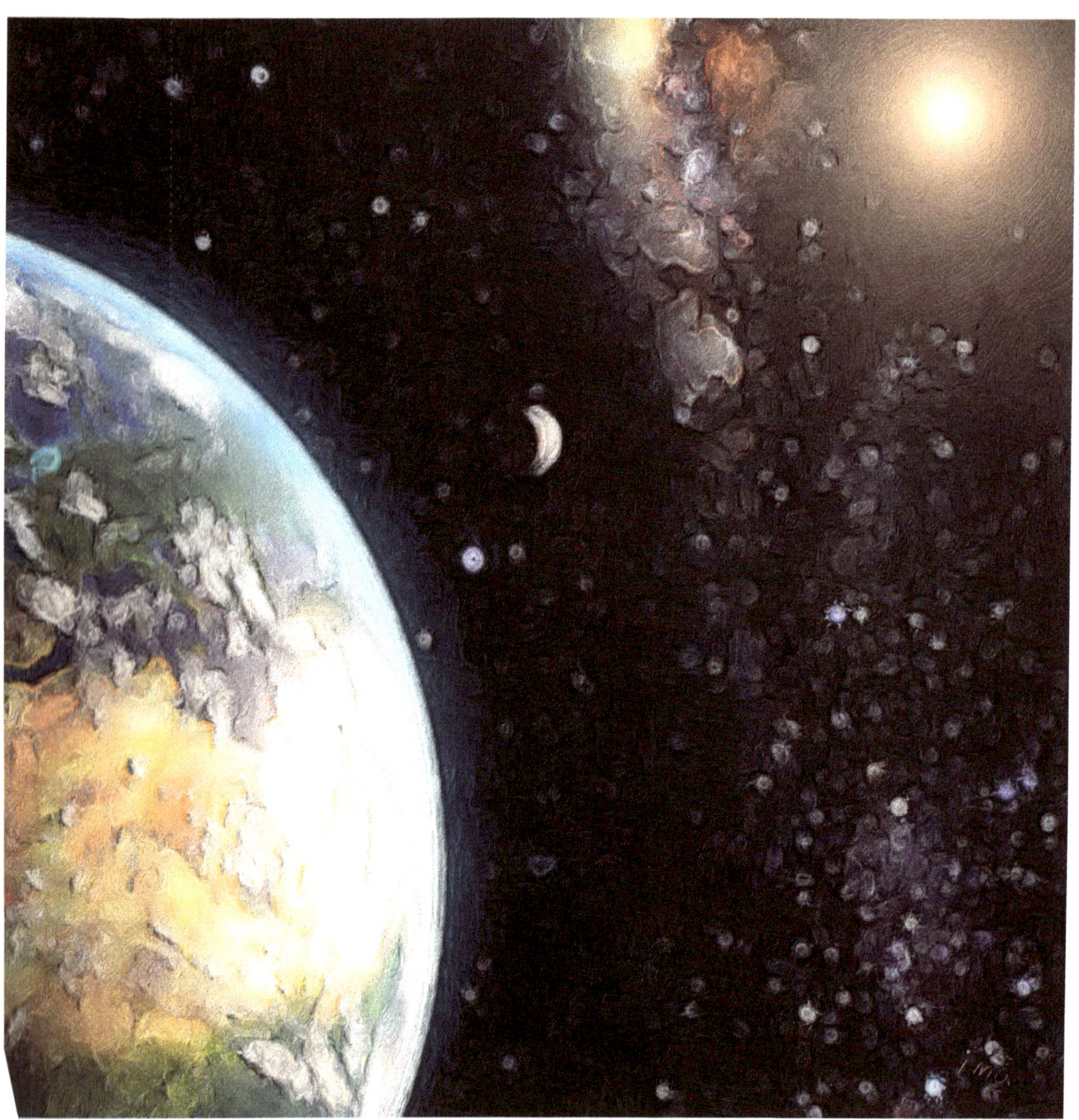

The spin was to remain. Conservation, kindness, goodwill, compassion, altruism, empathy, blessings, prayers, and the courage to be all these might be our saving Grace.
Those in tune with preserving the natural wonder are acknowledged as the knights and saints of God's perpetual wish.

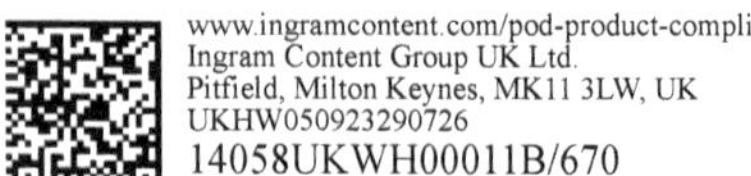
www.ingramcontent.com/pod-product-compliance
Ingram Content Group UK Ltd.
Pitfield, Milton Keynes, MK11 3LW, UK
UKHW050923290726
14058UKWH00011B/670